A LOOK AT U.S. ELECTIONS

THE HISTORY OF POLITICAL PARTIES

BY KATHRYN WESGATE

Gareth Stevens
PUBLISHING

CRASHCOU

The John P. Holt Brentwood Library
8109 Concord Road
Brentwood, TN 37027
Phone: 615-371-0090

Please visit our website, www.garethstevens.com. For a free color catalog of all our high-quality books, call toll free 1-800-542-2595 or fax 1-877-542-2596.

Library of Congress Cataloging-in-Publication Data
Names: Wesgate, Kathryn, author.
Title: The history of political parties / Kathryn Wesgate.
Description: New York : Gareth Stevens Publishing, [2021] | Series: A look at U.S. elections | Includes bibliographical references and index.
Identifiers: LCCN 2019047924 | ISBN 9781538259481 (library binding) | ISBN 9781538259467 (paperback) | ISBN 9781538259474 (6 Pack) | ISBN 9781538259498 (ebook)
Subjects: LCSH: Political parties--United States--History--Juvenile literature.
Classification: LCC JK2261 .W47 2021 | DDC 324.273--dc23
LC record available at https://lccn.loc.gov/2019047924

First Edition

Published in 2021 by
Gareth Stevens Publishing
111 East 14th Street, Suite 349
New York, NY 10003

Copyright © 2021 Gareth Stevens Publishing

Editor: Kate Mikoley

Photo credits: Cover, pp. 1 Herbert Gehr/The LIFE Picture Collection/Getty Images; series art kzww/Shutterstock.com; series art (newspaper) MaryValery/Shutterstock.com; p. 5 Andrey_Popov/Shutterstock.com; p. 7 Mark Hayes/Shutterstock.com; p. 9 https://commons.wikimedia.org/wiki/File:Alexander_Hamilton_portrait_by_John_Trumbull_1806.jpg; p. 11 Charles Haire/Shutterstock.com; p. 12 https://en.wikipedia.org/wiki/File:Official_Presidential_portrait_of_Thomas_Jefferson_(by_Rembrandt_Peale,_1800)(cropped).jpg; p. 13 https://commons.wikimedia.org/wiki/File:Gilbert_Stuart_Williamstown_Portrait_of_George_Washington.jpg; p. 15 traveler1116/DigitalVision Vectors/Getty Images; p. 17 https://commons.wikimedia.org/wiki/File:Andrew_jackson_headFXD.jpg; p. 19 MPI/Archive Photos/Getty Images; p. 21 https://commons.wikimedia.org/wiki/File:Martin_Van_Buren_by_Mathew_Brady_c1855-58.jpg; p. 23 Buyenlarge/Archive Photos/Getty Images; p. 25 Popperfoto/Getty Images p. 27 Hill Street Studios/DigitalVision/Getty Images; p. 29 adamkaz/E+/Getty Images.

All rights reserved. No part of this book may be reproduced in any form without permission in writing from the publisher, except by a reviewer.

Printed in the United States of America

Some of the images in this book illustrate individuals who are models. The depictions do not imply actual situations or events.

CPSIA compliance information: Batch #CS20GS: For further information contact Gareth Stevens, New York, New York at 1-800-542-2595.

CONTENTS

Let's Party!	4
The First Parties	6
The Federalists	8
The Anti-Federalists	10
No-Party President	12
Making It Official	14
Breaking Up	16
Whigs and Democrats	18
Fall of the Whigs	20
Two Parties Pull Ahead	22
Ever Changing	26
Timeline of Major Political Parties	30
Glossary	31
For More Information	32
Index	32

Words in the glossary appear in **bold** type the first time they are used in the text.

LET'S PARTY!

Today, the United States has a two-party political system. This means most voters vote for one of two major, or main, political parties. In the United States these are the Democrats and the Republicans. However, things haven't always been this way.

Make the Grade

A political party is a group of people who are alike in their beliefs and ideas about government. Political parties work to have their members elected to, or voted into, government offices.

THE FIRST PARTIES

Political parties in the United States began to form in the late 1700s, around the time the **U.S. Constitution** was being written. A federal, or central, government was forming. People had different ideas about how much power that government should have.

Make the Grade

Before the Constitution went into effect, nine states had to **ratify** it. Meeting and talking about ratifying it caused early political parties to form.

THE FEDERALISTS

Those in favor of the Constitution were called Federalists. They liked the idea of having a strong federal government that held much of the power. They thought it was important for the country to be joined together under this main government.

Make the Grade
The leader of the Federalists was Founding Father Alexander Hamilton.

9

THE ANTI-FEDERALISTS

Those in favor of a smaller federal government were known as the Anti-Federalists. They thought the Constitution gave the federal government too much power. As a result, they believed the states and people wouldn't have enough rights.

MAKE THE GRADE
The Anti-Federalists fought for the **Bill of Rights** to be added to the Constitution in order to give people more rights.

NO-PARTY PRESIDENT

As the first president, George Washington's **term** was unlike others in many ways. One of these ways was that he didn't officially stand for any one party. He did, however, tend to agree more often with the Federalists than the Anti-Federalists.

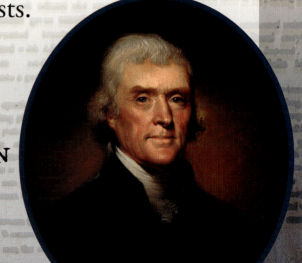

THOMAS JEFFERSON

Make the Grade
Washington's first **cabinet** included Hamilton, as well as Thomas Jefferson, who was an Anti-Federalist leader.

MAKING IT OFFICIAL

The Federalist Party officially formed in 1791, during Washington's first term in office. The **opposing** party, formed by Jefferson and James Madison, was first known as the Republican Party. It would later become known as the Democratic-Republican Party.

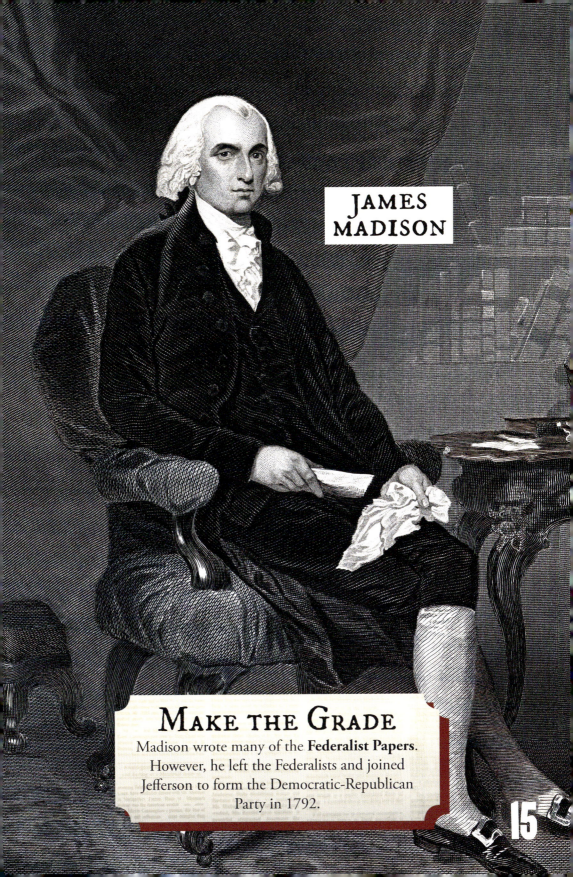

James Madison

Make the Grade

Madison wrote many of the **Federalist Papers**. However, he left the Federalists and joined Jefferson to form the Democratic-Republican Party in 1792.

BREAKING UP

The Federalists were in power until 1801, when Jefferson became president. The Democratic-Republicans held power until 1825. They then broke into two groups. One group was the National Republicans. By the 1830s, the National Republicans had helped form the Whig Party.

Make the Grade

Andrew Jackson, who became president in 1829, led the party that opposed the National Republicans. They were known as Jacksonian Democrats, or sometimes just Democrats.

WHIGS AND DEMOCRATS

The Whig Party officially formed in 1834. They thought Jackson acted more like a ruler than a president. In 1844, the Democratic Party became the official name of Jackson's party. They won all but two presidential elections from 1828 until 1856.

MAKE THE GRADE

The Whig Party got its name from an English political party that was against having kings and queens hold all the power. The Whigs nicknamed Jackson "King Andrew."

FALL OF THE WHIGS

By the 1850s, the Whig Party fell apart and new parties formed. People disagreed on whether to allow **slavery** in the new land added to the United States. In 1854, the Republican Party formed. It included past northern Whigs who were against slavery spreading to the new land.

MARTIN VAN BUREN

Make the Grade
Also in the new Republican Party were some past Democrats and members of the Free-Soil Party, a short-lived party against the spread of slavery that included past president Martin Van Buren.

TWO PARTIES PULL AHEAD

In 1860, Democrats had trouble. Southern Democrats thought slavery should be allowed in all areas, or territories, of the new land. Democrats from the North thought people in the new territories should decide for themselves if slavery was allowed.

Make the Grade

Republicans **nominated** Abraham Lincoln for president. Democrats in the North and South each nominated a **candidate**. Another party did too. With Democrats split, Lincoln easily won.

After Lincoln's election, it became clear the Democrats and Republicans were the two most powerful parties. This is still true today. However, the two parties continued to change in the years since Lincoln's election—and are still changing today!

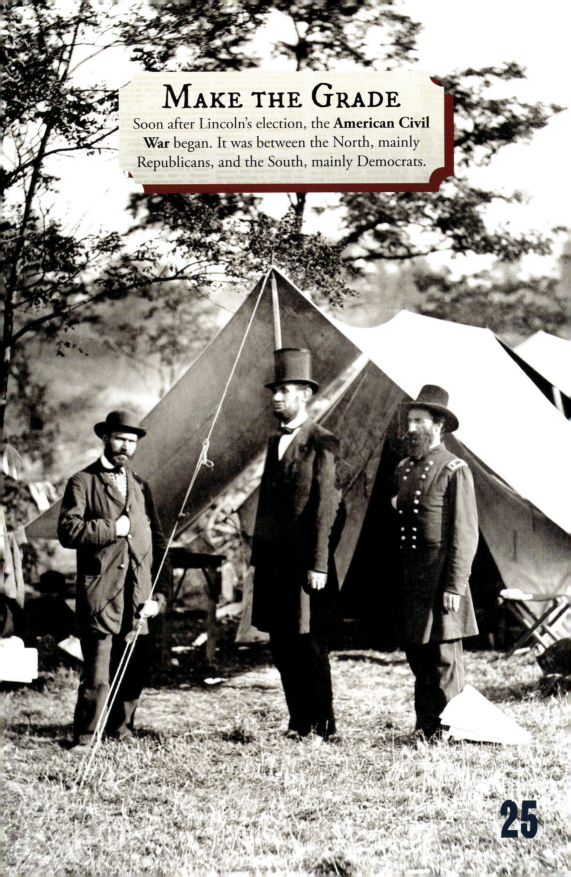

MAKE THE GRADE

Soon after Lincoln's election, the **American Civil War** began. It was between the North, mainly Republicans, and the South, mainly Democrats.

25

EVER CHANGING

By the middle of the 1900s, both the Democratic and Republican parties had gone through big changes. These two parties can get confusing, because the party that we call the Democrats today actually grew from Jefferson and Madison's party called the Republicans.

MAKE THE GRADE

While the Democrats and Republicans are still the two biggest parties in our system today, we also have many smaller parties.

There have been parties with "Democrat" or "Republican" in their name for hundreds of years. What was once considered a Democratic or Republican value may not fit the party's beliefs today. As time goes on, it's likely our political parties will continue to grow and change.

Make the Grade
By the time you're old enough to vote, it's possible these parties will have changed even more. Maybe there will even be a new political party!

TIMELINE OF MAJOR POLITICAL PARTIES

1791
The Federalist Party forms.

1792
The Democratic-Republican Party forms.

C. 1829
Democratic-Republicans start to call themselves Democrats.

1834
The Whig Party forms.

1844
Democratic-Republicans officially change their name to the Democratic Party.

1854
The Republican Party forms.

1860
Lincoln is elected, bringing forth the Democrats and Republicans as the country's two major parties.

GLOSSARY

American Civil War: a war fought from 1861 to 1865 in the United States between the Northern states and the Southern states

Bill of Rights: the first 10 amendments to the U.S. Constitution, which includes promises of individual rights and of limits on federal and state governments

cabinet: a group of senior officials appointed by the president as special advisors

candidate: a person who is running for office

Federalist Papers: a series of writings to newspapers in the 1780s aimed at getting voters to support ratifying the U.S. Constitution

nominate: to choose someone for a job or position

opposing: fighting or competing against another person or group

ratify: to give formal approval to something

slavery: the state of being owned by another person and forced to work without pay

term: the length of time a person holds a government or official office

U.S. Constitution: the piece of writing that states the laws of the United States

FOR MORE INFORMATION

BOOKS
Bjornlund, Lydia. *Modern Political Parties*. Minneapolis, MN: Core Library, 2017.

Martin, Bobi. *What Are Elections?* New York, NY: Britannica Educational Publishing in association with Rosen Educational Services, 2016.

WEBSITES

Bill of Rights
www.dkfindout.com/us/more-find-out/what-does-politician-do/bill-rights/
Read more about the Bill of Rights on this interactive website.

US Government: Two-Party System
www.ducksters.com/history/us_government/two-party_system.php
Learn more about the United States' two-party system here.

Publisher's note to educators and parents: Our editors have carefully reviewed these websites to ensure that they are suitable for students. Many websites change frequently, however, and we cannot guarantee that a site's future contents will continue to meet our high standards of quality and educational value. Be advised that students should be closely supervised whenever they access the Internet.

INDEX

Anti-Federalists 10, 11, 12, 13
Democratic Party 18, 26, 30
Democratic-Republican Party 14, 15, 16, 30
Democrats 4, 17, 18, 21, 22, 23, 24, 25, 26, 27, 28, 30
Federalist Party 14, 30
Federalists 8, 9, 12, 15, 16
Hamilton, Alexander 9, 13
Jackson, Andrew 17, 18, 19
Jefferson, Thomas 12, 13, 14, 15, 16, 26
Lincoln, Abraham 23, 24, 25, 30
Madison, James 14, 15, 26
Republican Party 14, 20, 21, 26, 30
Republicans 4, 16, 17, 23, 24, 25, 26, 27, 28, 30
Van Buren, Martin 21
Washington, George 12, 13, 14
Whig Party 16, 18, 19, 20, 30